SAYING GRACE

MEALTIME PRAYERS

Pray as often as you eat

GREG PEARCE

a. Acorn Press

Published by Acorn Press
An imprint of Bible Society Australia
ACN 148 058 306 | Charity licence 19 000 528
GPO Box 4161
Sydney NSW 2001
Australia

www.acornpress.net.au | www.biblesociety.org.au

ISBN 978-0-647-53336-9

First published by Morning Star Publishing in 2017,
ISBN 9780648208105

Cataloguing-in-Publication entry is available from the National Library of Australia http:/catalogue.nla.gov.au/.

A catalogue record for this
work is available from the
National Library of Australia

Cover and text design and layout by John Healy

Saying Grace

Quoting his Bible, Jesus said, "People do not live on bread alone." Nevertheless most of us eat more frequently than we pray.

If that is true, then fundamentally we are still hungry. We have a hunger that cannot be satisfied by food, not even by all the cooking shows we can access.

Judged by the number of cooking shows on TV, eating must surely be one of the highest rating pleasures of being human. Even looking at food seems to enrapture people. Preparing it is a great art form, though not one in which I excel.

If we eat and do not pray we may be fortunate gluttons but we will miss the best taste of all.

These prayers are designed to help. They come out of the happy Christian practice we call "saying grace", giving thanks to God every time we eat.

As I have read my Bible I have kept in mind themes like food, meals, hospitality, God's provision and our thanksgiving for it. It has led me to reflections that have surprised, delighted and occasionally troubled me, reflections about God's rich purpose for us and the whole teeming creation in which we live. The promise of the kingdom is woven into it all. These thoughts have turned to prayers, the graces you can say, with little adaptation, either together or alone.

This book is a revision and expansion of an earlier book, *Time Out: Mealtime Prayers*. In offering it in a new form I pray that it will enrich you as much as it has me in preparing it, that the life of God may be even more the central pleasure of our lives.

Greg Pearce

Jesus makes himself known

When he was at the table with them he took bread, gave thanks, broke it and began to give it to them. Then their eyes were opened and they recognised him, and he disappeared from their sight.

Luke 24:30-31

Jesus wants to open our eyes to see him, our ears to hear him and our whole lives to live with him.

Let's pray

Thank you, dear Lord Jesus. It is so good that we can eat and drink together, with you at the head of the table. Now you are with us as you ate with those first disciples after you rose from the dead.

The party spirit

The Son of Man came eating and drinking, and they say, "He is a glutton and a drunkard, a friend of tax collectors and sinners."

Matthew 11:19

Jesus really enjoyed himself. He invited all types of people to his table because God's kingdom is an invitation to a welcome home party.

Let's pray

Lord Jesus, you have joined us sinners for this meal. You love being human. You enjoy human company. You thrive on our friendship. May we enjoy God's company half as much as you enjoy ours.

Eat and drink deeply

Martha was distracted by all the preparations that had to be made... "Martha, Martha," the Lord said, "you are worried and upset about many things, but few things are needed – or indeed only one."

Luke 10:40-42

You see everything differently when you know Jesus is with us. Nothing else matters quite as much as it did.

Let's pray

Lord, thank you that we can eat this meal with you. It reminds us that you have called us friends. We are very lucky. We are blessed.

When we make our living

When you are harvesting in your field and you overlook a sheaf, do not go back to get it. Leave it for the foreigner, the fatherless and the widow, so that the Lord your God may bless you in all the work of your hands.

Deuteronomy 24:19

When we make a living for ourselves and our families God wants us, as a normal part of our lives, to provide for those who cannot support themselves.

Let's pray

Father, we thank you that you give to us so generously. We enjoy good food. It is your kindness toward us. Even as we eat this meal, give us a passion to share our good things with others.

The fruitful Spirit

God's love has been poured out into our hearts through the Holy Spirit, who has been given to us.

Romans 5:5

The Spirit of God produces fruit in us. Good fruit is delicious. It is tasty. It is sweet. It suits us very well, and we are the better for it.

Let's pray

Dear Father, we really enjoy the love you have poured upon us. This meal is one way. Your Spirit is another. And the one is like the other because both satisfy us. Both make us more complete and easier for others to get on with.

I have everything I need

The LORD is my shepherd. I lack nothing.
Psalm 23:1

I quite easily complain (to myself, at least) that I'm hard done by. Until, that is, I remember that God knows me by name and is ready to guide me, every step, and provide for me, every day.

Let's pray

Truly, Lord, you are my shepherd. I live under your watchful eye. You know me. You provide for me. This meal is the provision of the shepherd for his sheep, and I thank you.

Quiet Waters

He makes me lie down in green pastures,
he leads me beside quiet waters.

Psalm 23:2

*Mealtime is a chance to rest and to
be refreshed. Rest here. Be at peace.
Relax in the presence of God.*

Let's pray

Good Shepherd, make this meal a
stopping place with you. Thank you for
this time and this place to stop. Thank
you that I will get up again, satisfied and
refreshed.

Refreshment and direction

He refreshes my soul.
He guides me along the right paths
for his name's sake.

Psalm 23:3

*Confusion wearies us. When we do not
know who we are or what we are to do
we become worn out. Knowing God's
right paths for our lives is bracing and
renewing.*

Let's pray

Dear Lord, we need more than this meal
to refresh us: give us a moment to pause,
to remember you, and to find your way
for our lives. Then our souls will be
refreshed. For all this we thank you.

God prepares our table

You prepare a table before me
in the presence of my enemies.
You anoint my head with oil;
my cup overflows.

Psalm 23:5

*There is no place I can go where God
cannot reach me. In war, in prison, in
rejection by those I trusted, I never eat
alone.*

Let's pray

Dear Lord, I eat my meal in quiet joy
because wherever I am you reach me. You
prepare the table. You notice each one,
and give each a special touch. I thank you
that you include me.

Bread for the day

Give us today our daily bread.

Matthew 6:11

This is Jesus' prayer. The Lord's prayer. It's Israel's prayer on the journey through the wilderness: bread enough for today. It doesn't ask for too much. It's a desire to be simple and trusting.

Let's pray

Dear Father, your eye is upon us, the Father caring for your children. So we take up this food. It is our daily bread. We will eat it giving you thanks and praise, trusting you on our life's journey.

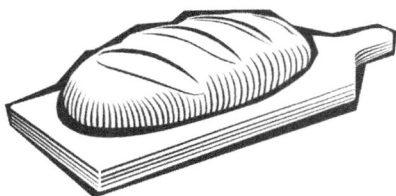

All the days of my life

Surely your goodness and love will follow me all the days of my life, and I will dwell in the house of the LORD forever.

Psalm 23:6

As you prepare to eat, stop to name one sign of God's goodness and love to you.

Let's pray

Dear Lord, your goodness and love are spread out before me in this meal. They are also spread out as I lay my life open before you. You have promised to be good to me forever; kind to me forever; Jesus has promised me a place in your house forever, and I thank you.

A world brimful

How many are your works, LORD!
In wisdom you have made them all;
the earth is full of your creatures.

Psalm 104:24

*The whole world of nature is our sister:
it comes from the hand of God as we
do. It never fails to delight, and from it
we glean our food.*

Let's pray

Poet and painter, sculptor and gardener:
you have produced a world brimful. We
love it. Thank you for all the plants and
creatures we enjoy, and for those who
have delivered our food.

Friends in deed

Suppose a brother or sister is without clothes and daily food. If one of you says to them, "Go in peace; keep warm and well fed," but does nothing about their physical needs what good is it?

James 2:15-16

Maybe, just maybe, there is someone who comes to mind who needs the help we can give today.

Let's pray

Father, when we have pleasant homes and stylish clothes; when our food satisfies, we must thank you. We are contented. But in case we should ever be complacent, give us an unquiet heart, and a way to help those who cannot sit down to a meal like this.

Our part in a world of praise

Let everything that has breath praise the
LORD.
Praise the LORD.

Psalm 150:6

*The whole creation is the theatre of
God's glory. All life gives praise to the
living God.*

Let's pray

We praise you, Father. You give every
breath we draw, every mouthful of food,
all the energy we have. Each ability comes
from you. We praise you. We glorify you.
We thank you.

The one at the door

Here I am! I stand at the door and knock.
If anyone hears my voice and opens the
door, I will come in and eat with them,
and they with me.

Revelation 3:20

*Jesus knocks at every door of every
life and every church. Even as we
prepare to eat this meal, make a place
for him to be part of our thoughts and
conversation.*

Let's pray

Welcome, Lord Jesus, as our mealtime
guest. You may take any chair. You may
sit with each of us. You may figure in our
thoughts and be on our minds as we talk
to each other. Be our leader in prayer:
bring our thanks before your Father and
our Father.

By the rivers, in the mountains

Let the rivers clap their hands,
let the mountains sing together for joy;
let them sing before the LORD.

Psalm 98:8-9

*Think of a favourite holiday spot by
a river, high up in the mountains, or
down in peaceful valleys. Even the
quiet is a song of praise to God.*

Let's pray

Lord, the rivers flow; the mountains
stand; the pleasant valleys fold
themselves away. They sing your songs.
They pray in silence. What you do is
wonderful. We too offer thanks and praise
for our meal.

The greatest of all banquets

One of those at table said to Jesus,
"Blessed are those who will eat at the
feast of the kingdom of God."

Luke 14:15

*The invitation to the banquet of the
kingdom is more important than any
other priority. All our activities are to
be assessed in the light of it. All our
meals are an anticipation of it.*

Let's pray

Dear Lord, you invite us to the greatest of
all banquets. There will be laughter. There
will be fellowship. It will be a reverend
and impossible privilege to be in your
presence. Thank you that we can have a
tiny anticipation of all this is this meal.

Show me your ways

Show me your ways, LORD,
teach me your paths.
Guide me in your truth and teach me,
for you are God my Saviour,
and my hope is in you all day long.

Psalm 25:4-5

*I have been given all the day long in
which to live. I eat this meal to sustain
me, to get me through the day. Let
me not waste it by turning away from
God's path down some pointless track.*

Let's pray

Dear Father, you are a mighty source of
power. You give me energy for each day,
and this meal reminds me of it. I thank
you for re-charging me, and I ask you to
turn all my energy into the ways you want
me to go.

Enough and to share

When you harvest the grapes in your vineyard, do not go over the vines again. Leave what remains for the foreigner, the fatherless and the widow.

Deuteronomy 24:21

If you think about it you will know that there are people who could use for necessities what we spend on luxuries.

Let's pray

Dear Lord, as we eat this meal we thank you humbly for daily food, a nightly bed, weekly entertainment and annual holidays. We are so grateful. We also ask that you open our hearts to those who struggle for these things, even for their daily food.

The community of creation

All creatures look to you
to give them their food at the proper time.
When you give it to them,
they gather it up;
when you open your hand,
they are satisfied with good things.

Psalm 104:27-28

We are a part of the whole community
of creation that looks to God and
depends upon God.

Let's pray

Living Lord, you have placed us in such
good company, the fellowship of the whole
creation. You feed us all. We speak for
all creatures who have no voice. For all
humble creatures who live in simplicity
we give you thanks for our daily food.

The Lord who kneels before us

Jesus got up from the meal, took off his outer clothing, and wrapped a towel around his waist. After that he poured water into a basin and began to wash his disciples' feet, drying them with the towel that was wrapped around him.

John 13:4-5

Surely it would be almost painful to see Jesus so humble before us, washing our feet before this meal.

Let's pray

Lord Jesus Christ, you are the ruler of the universe. All things have been made through you and for you. Yet you come to us on your knees. You have given your whole life to wash us clean. Prepare us to eat humbly and thankfully, and to serve each other all our days.

The kind father

As a father has compassion on his children, so the LORD has compassion on those who fear him.

Psalm 103:13

Who is it who has most kindly nurtured you? Who has provided for you and protected you? They have been God's hand toward you.

Let's pray

Father, we thank you for all the forms of your love, for the guiding hand, for strong comfort and for those who have fed and clothed us as we grew. We celebrate your kindness now in the butter on the bread and the smile on each other's face.

From the farmers' market

He makes grass grow for the cattle,
and plants for people to cultivate –
bringing forth food from the earth:
wine that gladdens human hearts,
oil to make their faces shine,
and bread that sustains their hearts.

Psalm 104:14-15

*Ploughing, planting, breeding, herding,
fishing, harvesting, processing, bottling,
distributing, selling the food, shopping
for it and preparing it: this table before
us has taken so much human activity.*

Let's pray

Father, we must be grateful at so many
levels for this meal. We are part of others
and they are part of us. We all depend
on each other and we all depend on you.
All praise and thanks for your rich, full
goodness.

Don't go thirsty

Those who drink the water I give them will never thirst. Indeed, the water I give them will become in them a spring of water welling up to eternal life.

John 4:14

Jesus diagnosed our condition: endlessly thirsty, with a thirst beyond any possible satisfaction (unless we let the second best substitute for the real thing.) No, we are made for him, to be satisfied by him alone.

Let's pray

Our food, our drink satisfies us until the next meal, or maybe only until the next snack. Yet we thank you for it, dear Lord. We really do. But you promise something much deeper, living water, and we thank you that this comes from you giving yourself.

The special privilege of eating with Jesus

He was not seen by all the people, but by witnesses whom God had already chosen – by us who ate and drank with him after he rose from the dead.

Acts 10:41

We can base our lives on the apostles' report: Jesus, risen from death, met them in a meal. He lives to eat with us by faith, and that is a promise that one day we will eat and drink with him in God's Kingdom.

Let's pray

Lord Jesus, you came to your deserted followers as a friend. You ate and drank and talked with them. Thank you that you come to us too. Now every taste of our food is a fore-taste of your kingdom to come.

The needy and the greedy

God will never forget the needy;
the hope of the afflicted will never
perish.

Psalm 9:18

*This is an often repeated theme: God
looks with care on the needy. We can
only be the true people of God when we
build this into our lifestyle.*

Let's pray

Dear Lord, we give thanks for our meal.
We have it through your kindness to us.
Let our hearts be open in kindness to
others and closed to greed in ourselves.

The pleasure of slow foods

Be patient, then, brothers and sisters, until the Lord's coming. See how the farmer waits for the land to yield its valuable crop, patiently waiting for the autumn and spring rains.

James 2:7

Anticipation whets the appetite. When the long-awaited meal arrives it makes the waiting so much more worthwhile. And that's a spiritual lesson.

Let's pray

Our food is ready for us. Father, thank you for our appetite. Thank you for the pleasure of anticipation. May we taste your goodness until our lives come to their end and we sit down, deeply satisfied, at the banquet of the Lord.

Our day's work

Then people go out to work,
to their labour until evening.

Psalm 104:23

*Work is good and satisfying, at least
the outcome of our work when it
provides for us. It's good if we do the
work. It's good when we get the benefit
of someone else's honest work.*

Let's pray

God our provider, this is your world and it
supports us all when we respect everyone
in it. Thank you for those who have
worked in order that we may eat today.
Thank you for our meal.

The company Jesus keeps

While Jesus was having dinner at Levi's house many tax collectors and sinners were eating with him and his disciples, for there were many who followed him.

Mark 2:15

Jesus invites everyone to eat with him, and everyone comes as a sinner, asking to be forgiven. In fact we depend upon being forgiven. So there are no barriers when we sit with him, and we have a lot of fun.

Let's pray

Lord Jesus, all company with you is good company. All meals with you are special celebrations. Thank you for this meal and for one another at the table.

Thanks for good seasons

They sowed fields and planted vineyards
that yielded a fruitful harvest;
he blessed them, and their numbers
greatly increased,
and he did not let their herds diminish.

Psalm 107:37-38

*Picture the land under crop and
orchard, the rains in season, the
maturing sun to swell the mellow
fruitfulness, the machines and the
workforce heading out to harvest.*

Let's pray

Thank you, Father, for this rich earth, the
seasons conspiring on our behalf, loading
up and blessing sheds and fridges and
pantries with fruit and produce. We are
the end product. We can eat our fill. It is
lovely.

Hidden food

"My food," said Jesus, "is to do the will of him who sent me and to finish his work."

John 4:34

Our food is to give us energy, but nothing gives energy and vitality quite as much as knowing what God has for us to do. This is our vocation.

Let's pray

Lord Jesus, we can see that it truly nourished you to participate in the Father's plans. How we pray for that also. We thank you for this meal and we pray that we will get up from it ready to do your Father's will.

From the good earth

Then God said, "I give you every seed-bearing plant on the face of the whole earth and every tree that has fruit with seed in it. They will be yours for food."

Genesis 1:29

What we can eat we give thanks for. Of all the plants we cannot eat, some can shade or shelter us, some clothe us, some intrigue us, and some we find downright beautiful. It's all so glorious.

Let's pray

Our great Creator, you give us all kinds of plants for food: grains, vegetables, fruits and berries. And many more to delight us, and some even to decorate our tables. All come from your good earth, and we thank you.

Making room for others

When you beat the olives from your trees, do not go over the branches a second time. Leave what remains for the foreigner, the fatherless and the widow.

Deuteronomy 24:20

There's something at the core of our lives that must spill over into generosity to others. We have been blessed. When we know it deeply we will find ways to put others in a better place.

Let's pray

Dear Lord, thank you that you are so generous to us. We receive this meal with grateful hearts. You give us more than we need. Help us to find and know and follow our way to meet the needs of others.

Give thanks whatever

Give thanks in all circumstances; for this is God's will for you in Christ Jesus.

1 Thessalonians 5:18

Give thanks in all things? Even if the dinner's burnt? The food's gone off? In fact there are far worse things than these, and Christians have had to live through them. So, whatever it is for you today: give thanks!

Let's pray

Father, we thank you for Jesus and all he went through for us. We thank you through Jesus: he brings us to you. We thank you in all circumstances, because he knows our life and times and we cannot be separated from him. And of course we thank you for this meal.

I will sing

I will sing to the LORD all my life;
I will sing praise to my God as long as
I live.

Psalm 104:33

*Whatever the quality of your voice, if
you love God and you want to express
it, your whole life will become a song of
praise.*

Let's pray

Lord, I want to sing your praise. I want
to thank you for your loving kindness. I
thank you for tenderly counting my days.
I thank you for the meal before me now:
it is my daily bread. I thank you that I am
blessed by the God of the universe as I
eat and drink. How good my life is.

The breakfast that is never over

When they landed they saw a fire of burning coals there with fish on it, and some bread. Jesus said to them, "Come and have breakfast."

John 21:9,12

Jesus is risen. He's alive. He wants to eat and drink with us. He wants us to come along with him as his followers and even as his friends. And he does not want this to ever end.

Let's pray

Lord, we thank you because you wish us never to be away from your company. We only harm ourselves if we try to be. Let us eat with you, listen to you and walk with you. We are the guests at your meal.

Spring waters

He makes springs pour water into the
ravines;
it flows between the mountains.
They give water to all the beasts of the
field;
the wild donkeys quench their thirst.

Psalm 104:10-11

Mealtime is like a watering hole
in the valleys. It gives us rest and
refreshment.

Let's pray

Lord, you give us water for our thirst
and food for our hunger. You refresh our
comrades the animals, and, of all your
creatures, we are the ones who can give
you thanks.

World cuisine: the ultimate banquet

People will come from east and west and north and south and will take their places in at the feast in the kingdom of God.

Luke 13:29

We all have our favourite cuisines: Indian, Thai, Lebanese, fish and chips or Mum's cooking. Imagine the menu when, with all our varied and educated tastes, God is the host of all the peoples of the earth. He has been planning this all along!

Let's pray

How exciting it is to sit down to a well planned meal. We thank you for the fun of it, dear Lord. We thank you for the promise of a great feast to come, too, with such delightful and varied company. You promise us more than we can ask or think.

When we need faith for each day

They asked, and he brought them quail; he fed them well with the bread of heaven.

Psalm 105:40

Imagine that all around is barren bush land, no settled farms. We are the people of God and we are passing through. And God says we will be fed each day.

Let's pray

God our provider, we depend on you as much as Israel did in the wilderness. But we forget it. We depend on you right now, every second, every day and night. Thank you for feeding us. Thank you for this meal, your provision for each day.

Drawing up our guest list

When you give a banquet invite the poor,
the crippled, the lame, the blind, and you
will be blessed. Although they cannot
repay you, you will be repaid at the
resurrection of the righteous.

Luke 14:13-14

*As we eat today here is a topic for
thought: who can I invite in the future?
What? When? Where? I mean in the
light of Jesus' idea of a good party.*

Let's pray

Dear Lord, thank you for this meal.
Thank you for parties and special
celebrations. Thank you for those you
have marked out as friends I could make
into the future, even guests for a meal.

A cup of cold water

If anyone gives even a cup of cold water to one of these little ones who is known to be my disciple, truly I tell you, that person will certainly be rewarded.

Matthew 10:42

Jesus expects us to be hospitable. He accepted hospitality when he went on mission. He expects that those who go to new places at his call and direction will be supported by the faithful community.

Let's pray

Thank you, dear Lord, for all the times we have been welcomed with warm hospitality. Thank you for this meal and all meals of welcome. Give us the privilege of supporting those on mission in your name.

An open table

Do not forget to show hospitality to strangers, for by so doing some people have shown hospitality to angels without knowing it.

Hebrew 13:2

Just now and then we will get to know someone for the first time and we think, "You were sent by God."

Let's pray

Loving God, thank you for meals where new friendships grow. Thank you for relationships that form as we eat and talk. For meals in restaurants and in parks. May our table be open to whoever you will bring.

Bread of Life

Jesus declared, "I am the bread of life. Whoever comes to me will never go hungry, and whoever believes in me will never be thirsty."

John 6:35

We have a hunger at this time that food can soon fix. But there is a deep hunger for a real relationship of love, and we will starve unless that hunger is satisfied.

Let's pray

Lord Jesus, thank you for bread. Thank you for daily bread. Thank you for this meal. Our deeper hunger never goes away. You are the real satisfaction for that. Take our empty lives and fill them with all the fullness of God.

Thanksgiving for God's compassion

He has caused his wonders to be
remembered;
the Lord is gracious and compassionate.
He provides food for those who fear him;
he remembers his covenant forever.

Psalm 111:4-5

*The practice of worship, the habit of
thanksgiving, the pattern of stopping
before a meal to remember God's
loving-kindness - for those who do
these things, simply and faithfully,
their lives become like a prayer.*

Let's pray

Dear Lord, we pause before we eat
to declare your loving-kindness and
to thank you. Because we know who
provides for us, even the meal itself is
that much more precious.

Ransomed, healed, restored, forgiven

Praise the LORD, my soul;
all my inmost being, praise his holy name.
Praise the LORD, my soul,
and forget not all his benefits.

Psalm 103:1-2

God's benefits, this psalm declares, include forgiveness and healing and lifting our lives out of their rut, renewal in body and soul.

Let's pray

Lord, when we bless you we somehow are blessed ourselves. When we bless you for our health and strength we are further blessed in health and strength. So for our food we say, "Bless the Lord, my soul, all my inmost being, all that is within me. Bless the Lord."

The rhythm of the seasons

He made the moon to mark the seasons,
and the sun knows when to go down.

Psalm 104:19

*The rhythm of the seasons does it. All
the rhythms of our lives do it. If we
fall into some regular routine at meal
time that does it too: it tells us that the
mercy of God comes to us new and
fresh again and again.*

Let's pray

God of the seasons, the sun and the
moon that go through their phases:
the rains gather after drought and
drench the hills and plains. Then our
food comes again. The patterns of our
lives renew us, and we give thanks at
this mealtime.

Jesus invites himself in

When Jesus reached the spot, he looked up and said to him, "Zacchaeus, come down immediately. I must stay at your house today."

Luke 19:5

The art and practice of being a Christian involves recognising that Jesus says the same surprising and transforming words to us as he said to Zacchaeus.

Let's pray

Friend of sinners, you re-make our sinful lives when you come home to us. As unready as we are, make this your home today, and re-make us. We thank you for being so humbly present at our meal.

The fellowship meal

They devoted themselves to the apostles'
teaching and to fellowship, to the
breaking of bread and to prayer.

Acts 2:42

*The Holy Spirit poured out on the first
Christians turned them into a highly
attractive community. They naturally
ate together and others wanted to join
them.*

Let's pray

Thank you, Father, for your Spirit poured
out upon us. Your Spirit brings us
together. Thank you for food to share. It is
a real sign of love among us. Let there be
no need among us that another can meet.

Happiness

Glory in his holy name;
let the hearts of those who seek the LORD
rejoice.

Psalm 105:3

*Real, unlooked-for happiness is part of
the whole deal of giving praise to God.
We are not cheated by giving glory to
another, where it is really due. A happy
heart is a by-product.*

Let's pray

Your over-flowing goodness never stops
flowing over. Day by day we sit down to
good food, and we thank you, Lord. You
are the holy God of all creation and you
are our God.

The bread of God

The bread of God is the bread that comes down from heaven and gives life to the world.

John 6:33

Let each mouthful of this meal remind us of the true bread, the one who gives life to everyone and to each of us.

Let's pray

God our maker and our provider, true bread of heaven and earth, we thank you for every meal, every day. We are fed by your love, given life by your love, taste heaven on earth in your love.

The fruitful earth

He waters the mountains from his upper
chambers;
the land is satisfied by the fruit of his work.

Psalm 104:13

*Because it witnesses to its creator the
earth cannot help being pregnant with
life.*

Let's pray

Water of life, sweet flowing water, growing
life, you send the rain that swells the fruit
and grain so we can eat. And we can swell
too, and we can grow. Thank you for all
this. How good it is to live.

The good good Father

Which of you fathers, if your son asks for a fish, will give him a snake instead? If you, then, though you are evil, know how to give good gifts to your children, how much more will your Father in heaven give the Holy Spirit to those who ask him?

Luke 11:11,13

If you dare compare God with a cook or chef, be sure that he will set out before you much more than you ever expected.

Let's pray

Father, thank you that you know what is truly good for us: food to sustain us. But more, your Spirit anoints us. He beautifies us. In the Spirit we see your beauty. There is glory here in a meal.

Water in the desert

He opened the rock, and water gushed out; it flowed like a river in the desert.

Psalm 105:41

Imagine yourself in the desert in summer, in the heat, in the dry. It's thirsty country.

Let's pray

Thank you, God our provider, for rain when it pours, for rivers that ripple, for springs and bores; for town reservoirs, for pipelines and rainwater tanks; for seeds shooting, for good food and a cool drink and for getting up from the table refreshed.

For the life of the city

There he brought the hungry to live,
and they founded a city where they
could settle.

Psalm 107:36

*Think of all the different cultures drawn
together in a city, all the peoples. In
their foods they love to show off the
way they have been blessed, and they
often began as the dishes of the poor.*

Let's pray

God of the city, thank you for the choice
we have of every kind of food. For the
places we can eat and the people we
can meet. Thank you that meals shared
enrich our humanity.

Don't worry

I tell you, do not worry about your life, what you will eat or drink; or about your body, what you will wear. Is not life more important than food, and the body more important than clothes?

Matthew 6:25

What really and truly belongs to God we cannot lose. So if we really and truly belong to God, why worry? Really and truly?

Let's pray

God our loving Father, thank you for food, this meal; and for clothes, these we wear. And for life, this life that is in your hands. Our lives are yours. We cannot be lost to you. That is our peace.

The mystery guests

Abraham ran to the herd and selected
a choice, tender calf and gave it to a
servant, who hurried to prepare it. He
then brought some curds and milk and
the calf that had been prepared, and
set these before them. While they ate he
stood near them under a tree.

Genesis 18:7-8

Abraham and Sarah hosted three
strangers, a long slow meal. It was the
Lord they welcomed. He promised them
a future for themselves and the world.
This was a life-changing meal for more
than themselves.

Let's pray

Thank you, Lord, that you are as present
at this mealtime. Your presence is
freighted with promise. You do not leave
us without a future.

Prayers for special mealtimes

Especially for children

He satisfies the thirsty
and fills the hungry with good things.

Psalm 107:9

Are you ready to eat?

Let's pray

Thanks for everything we drink
And for everything we chew.
Thanks for Jesus' words to think
About and Jesus' words to do.
(Psst! Just whisper now.)
And the dishes in the sink
Are for us to do, too.
THANK... YOU... LORD!

For a wedding

The kingdom of heaven is like a king who prepared a wedding banquet for his son.

Matthew 22:2

A marriage is our happiest celebration, so happy that it is like God's own kingdom, as joyful as that.

Let's pray

We praise you, living God, for a bride and bridegroom's love and for the promises they have made; for families and friends together; for old memories and the start of something new; for songs and laughter, firm good wishes, and eating until we're full. Thank you that a marriage feast is like your kingdom, and your kingdom is joy forever.

On a birthday

You created my inmost being;
you knit me together in my mother's
womb.
I praise you because I am fearfully and
wonderfully made;
your works are wonderful,
I know that full well.

Psalm 139:13-14

*It's a birthday. God knows us better
than we know ourselves, and God
delights in us.*

Let's pray

Thank you, Father, for a love so long and
deep that we were treasured even before
we were born. Thank you that others
delight in us, too. Thank you that we can
all enjoy this birthday meal with one of
your dear children.

When I eat alone

Where can I go from your Spirit?
Where can I flee from your presence?

Psalm 139:7

*Even when I am alone it can actually
be quite good. I can have space for
the unseen promised presence. I can
welcome the company of my advocate,
the Holy Spirit. The Spirit is also called
the paraclete, the one alongside.*

Let's pray

In your purpose, living God, when I am in
the Spirit I am also in your Son. Because
I am in the Son I am in the presence of
his Father. I'm hardly lonely at all! There
is a fellowship I share, the communion
of God. Even this meal before me is a
fellowship meal, and I thank you.

In the time of sorrow

For I eat ashes as my food
and mingle my drink with tears.

Psalm 102:9

*When sorrows come upon us, lonely
days and wretchedness, our appetite
seems to disappear. It's hard to make
much even of a good meal.*

Let's pray

Lord, we have known no sorrows like
your sorrows, no grief like your grief. You
tasted vinegar on the bitter cross. Thank
you for bearing and sharing our dark
times.

At the time of loss. After a funeral

Even though I walk through the darkest valley,
I will fear no evil,
for you are with me;
your rod and your staff, they comfort me.

Psalm 23:4

At the time of death a shadow falls. We lose a friend and we lose part of ourselves. But we do not lose the deepest part: God's near presence.

Let's pray

In the dark day be our light. In the lonely day be our friend. In the times we are falling apart hold on to us. In our isolation thank you that we are gathered to each other by this meal. Be with us in the kind word and the fond memory and the faithful hope.

Protest food: a kind of fast

John wore clothing made of camel's hair, with a leather belt around his waist, and he ate locusts and wild honey.

Mark 1:6

Jesus' cousin John could have had better to eat, and he could have joined Jesus in the conviviality Jesus was famous for. But he had a calling to live in protest against materialism and he did it this way.

Let's pray

Lord, when I fast let me be led by you.
Let me be led to listen to you.
Let me be in fellowship with those who have walked closely with you.
Let me address the needs of the world that sinks under its own indulgence.
Let me be unfailingly thankful that I do not live by bread alone but by every word that comes from the mouth of God.
Let me have a deep and renewing joy.

At Christmas

She gave birth to her firstborn, a son. She wrapped him in cloths and placed him in a manger, because there was no guest room available for them.

Luke 2:7

Christmas is a great celebration for us and the whole world. Make room for Jesus!

Let's pray

Lord Jesus, born in a stable, be born in our lives. Rejected by your own, be welcome at our table. You brought God into troubled city streets and villages and country houses. People could laugh again. Make this a happy time, too, and bless our Christmas meal.

On the first day of the week

On the first day of the week we came together to break bread.

Acts 20:7

Let's never fail to thank God on Sundays. This day we celebrate our own new life: it is the day Christ was raised from the dead.

Let's pray

We thank you, Lord, that we can break bread on this day. It is the day of your rising, the first born from among the dead, and hope for the whole world. We give thanks on the day Christians gather to hear your word, to greet each other, and to share communion with you, our risen Lord. Come among us, Lord Jesus.

Add your own graces

The approach I have taken has been
to begin with a verse of scripture
- themes are mentioned in the
introduction - to think about the
verse, and to pray out of that thought.
Lastly I have given it a title. It is a
fruitful pattern to follow in preparing
your own graces. There are a few
pages provided for you to follow this
form, and also pages to include graces,
your own or others', in other forms.

Title _____

Verse _____

_____

_____

_____

_____

Thought _____

_____

_____

_____

Prayer _____

_____

_____

_____

_____

_____

_____

_____

Title _____

Verse _____
_____
_____
_____
_____

Thought _____
_____
_____
_____

Prayer _____
_____
_____
_____
_____
_____
_____
_____

Title _____

Verse _____

_____

_____

_____

_____

_____

Thought _____

_____

_____

_____

_____

Prayer _____

_____

_____

_____

_____

_____

_____

_____

Title _____

Verse _____
_____
_____
_____
_____
_____

Thought _____
_____
_____
_____
_____

Prayer _____
_____
_____
_____
_____
_____
_____
_____

Graces

Graces

Graces

Graces